Introduction

Parlor games are games one plays at home among friends. A parlor game has no serious board or piece or other device which might get in the way of frivolity. There are no tournaments in parlor games. There are master players, but they are a modest lot and carry no trophies.

It is said that the parlor game was invented in Victorian England immediately upon the invention of the parlor. The Victorian parlor was a velvet chamber filled with horsehair sofas and strange lamps and suppressed sexual desire. It is said that the parlor game was invented to prevent one from thinking about what one was not allowed to think about and it was, of course, supremely successful — a thing so engaging, so inventive, so charming that primitive passions were kept in check.

Today — how shall I say it? — we have other things to keep under control. But parlor games are still an antidote to boredom, suitable when you are at the beach, in the woods, or in a great house with many bannisters. They are useful as well when one is asked to participate in whatever happens to be the striptease of the hour, when one longs for more formal days, days when there was such a thing as a parlor, and a game.

Parlor games are highly transportable. You can take them to picnics or dinner parties or to lunch. You simply fold them up neatly and file them in your frontal lobe, under "P" or "Reckless Gaiety" or "Things to do when the world turns sour."

Ghost, Hinkie Pinkie, and My Grandmother's Trunk are good for playing on long, dumb car trips. Two friends of mine once played Botticelli for fifty miles while lying in the back of a mule cart in Africa. This adventure, as well as the train wreck that led to it, was unplanned. Their combined competitiveness, however, kept her mind off her cracked ribs and his off his shattered ankle.

Lest you think that this book is merely a rehash of those old favorites, we might add that the couple could just as easily have played Deprivation or Zoom Schwartz Mordice — games to suit the decade. Both are included here, as well as Sexual Secrets, Guerrilla Scrabble, and Mental Strip Poker.

Finally, for those of you who are neither trendy nor decadent nor in pain, we include Wham and Paper Bag and Going Blank and Spoon. And many more — over fifty in all — to keep you occupied and content while the world breathes on around you.

San Francisco   N.G.
July 1979

Deprivation

The invention of a dear, martyred friend.

Number of players: Any number.

Tools: A box of toothpicks.

To win: Prove that you are the most deprived person in the room.

The play: Each person gets five toothpicks. Someone begins by declaring some lack in her life, e.g., "I have never been to Paris." Each player who has been to Paris must give the unfortunate one a toothpick. And so on, until someone gathers all the toothpicks and wins (or loses, as the case may be).

There are really three levels on which to play Deprivation. The first is fooling around, kid stuff: "I have never been on a pair of roller skates." The second is more advanced and may include throwaways like, "I have never danced with a nun." With that line, you don't get many toothpicks but you do get points for being clever. The third level is real adult play requiring chutzpah or idiocy or both: "I have never slept with my best friend's husband." At this level, most people lie.

Sardines

Sardines is a variation on Hide-and-Seek. It was played in Louis Malle's "Pretty Baby."

Number of players: A crowd.

Tools: A large house or hotel with many hiding places.

To win: Find the collective hiding place.

The play: All the players gather in one room. Then, one person — just one — leaves the room and hides somewhere. The rest give the old 50 count and then disperse to search. When a player finds the hidden person, she does not scream, "One, two, three on Joey Smith!" Instead, she joins that person — very, very quietly. As more players find the hiding place, they crowd in, until some poor fool is left wandering around in the lower foyer. The others can either wait three hours until they are found or scream and giggle and carry on, which is what they have been aching to do all along. The first person to find the hiding place gets to be the first one out on the next go-round.

You cannot practice or cheat, but you can arrange, through a complex series of winks, codes, and messages, to have a special friend hide with you.

9

Essence or Portraits

My favorite, a game that takes intuition and has a couple of nice variations.

Number of players: A fairly small dinner party is best.

Tools: None.

To win: Guess who the others have in mind.

The play: Send one person, IT, out of the room. Now decide on a person, living or dead, who is well known to the group. Let us say that the person is Carl Jung. Sit back and think about Jung's character for a little while. Then call IT back into the room.

IT begins questioning, phrasing the questions thus: "If I were a _____, what would I be?" A pedestrian example: "If I were a color, what color would I be?" In the case of Jung, I would answer, "Deep blue." Something about water and the unconscious. It's best not to think too much about the answers, but to let them flow, as they say. A better example: "If I were a sexual fantasy, what would I be?" For Jung, I would reply, "Being seduced by Freud." IT may ask the same question of everyone or change questions as she desires. The game goes on until IT guesses Jung's name.

Related Games

Rules: A variation on Essence. IT again leaves the room. But this time, the players decide on an imaginary game with one simple, underlying rule. The rule, for example, could be that IT's questions must be answered as though each player were the person to her immediate left. On the other hand, players may decide to answer IT's questions as though they were all Norman Mailer. Or every third answer might contain a number. Any very simple constant will do. IT comes back into the room and begins asking questions — any question except, "What is the rule for this game?" You may give IT as many clues as you like. The game ends when IT guesses the rule or something close to it.

Future: A variation on Rules. This time, with IT out of the room, the players imagine themselves to be people in a future in which one element of life has changed. For example: Money is no longer the medium of exchange, lines of poetry are; or people communicate only by exchanging recipes. ("Two cups diced chicken." "Whip until firm.") When IT returns, the group is engaged in acting out this scenario — preferably in small groups. In the case of the money, for example, two players might be doing a scene called "Deposit at the Bank." IT may ask questions (which should be answered in character), hover about, or simply watch. The game ends when IT has guessed what has changed.

To practice: Remember your high school drama days.

To cheat: It can't be done.

Pass the Orange

This is a really dumb game. Everybody thinks it's dumb. Kids think it's dumb. Parents think it's dumb. Even dogs find this game thoroughly stupid. But at night, when no one is looking, those same beings say to themselves, "Pass the Orange . . . Now that's a fun game in a dim-witted sort of way. . ."

Number of players: More than ten; more than twenty is even better.

Tools: Two Sunkist oranges from California.

To win: Pass the orange to the end of the line before the opposing team can do so.

The play: Divide into two teams. Each team lines up behind a leader, who is, by happenstance, holding an orange. Someone is designated the starter — Uncle Mort, who won't ever play — and he yells, "Go." At the sound of "Go," the leader places the orange under his chin and turns to the person behind him. The person behind him, known as the receiver, readies himself by placing his feet a couple of feet apart and maintaining that steady stance. He gestures to the leader with his neck and chin, rather like a courting swan. The leader assumes a like pose and tries, ever so gently, to place the orange under the chin of his teammate. Once the orange is rightly situated, the receiver grips it with his chin and attempts the same acrobatic on the person standing behind him. At no time can the hands be used! Even if the orange falls to the floor, it must be picked up with the chin of the person who dropped it. (You can have no pride in this game.)

The play continues until one team manages to get the orange to the end of its line. At that point it is pronounced the winner and everyone can sit down and have another martini.

To practice: Do neck-stretching exercises or watch courting swans.

To cheat: Hide an extra orange in your collar.

Botticelli

Botticelli is a literary game named after the 15th century Italian painter and having nothing to do with him. It is the king of parlor games. To play, you must have a great number of irrelevant names stored in your head and a retrieval system that rivals an IBM.

Number of players: Two or more.

Tools: A working knowledge of the alphabet.

To win: Remember the name of every famous person who has ever graced the earth.

The play: One person is designated IT. IT thinks of the name of a famous person, living or dead, or someone well known to the gathering. (IT may name ITself.) Reveal only the first letter of the famous person's surname. Let us say IT is thinking of Botticelli. IT says, "I am someone whose name begins with B." Now, going around the room clockwise, each person asks a question about a famous person whose name begins with B. For example: "Are you a German composer?" IT responds, "No, I am not Bach." The next person might ask, "Are you a 19th century woman poet?" IT answers, "No, I am not Elizabeth Barrett Browning." A real Botticelli fanatic might ask, "Are you a 20th century female painter who died in 1942?" IT responds something like "Barf." This is not an answer. Our fanatic must now say who she had in mind. "Cecilia Beaux," she says. Then she gets a free question. She can ask anything about the person at all. A good opener is the obvious, "Are you male or female?" IT responds, "Male."

The questions continue now as before except that they must all concern male famous people. Players ask questions designed to stump IT, getting free questions if they do, and thus narrow down the field until someone guesses correctly, on his turn, "BOTTICELLI, you dog."

There are a couple of wrinkles. First: IT may answer a question with any name that fits — it need not be the person the questioner had in mind. In the example of a German composer, IT could as well have answered, "Beethoven" or "Brahms." Thus, to stump IT you should be as specific as you can be in your questions. Second: There are those who say that free questions must be "yes or no" questions. In the example of male of female, they say you have to ask, "Is your person male?" This rule is horseshit.

To practice: Read the biographical list at the end of Webster's New Collegiate Dictionary.

To cheat: IT cannot lie about the original name because that would be dumb, as well as grounds for manslaughter. But both IT and the rest of the players can cheat throughout if they don't get caught. They can make up all manner of names and incredible biographies to go with them. Let your conscience be your guide.

Telephone

A grand game based on that most grand of pastimes, gossiping.

Number of players: The more, the better.

Tools: Gigantic ears and a wagging tongue.

To win: There is no winning in betrayal.

The play: The players gather in what amounts to a loose line, so that the ears of adjacent players are readily available. The person at one end of the line, it doesn't matter which, is designated the starter. He or she thinks up some clever line and whispers it to the adjoining player. Whatever the player hears, he then passes on to the next player, and so on until the play gets to the person at the end. That person then repeats, out loud, what he has just heard. You can imagine. . .

There are several ways to start the game. You may start with a line from Shakespeare and you will end, undoubtedly, with Harold Robbins; you can start with fairly innocent gossip and end with grounds for divorce. The game is not worth more than a few rounds, but those will be well spent.

To practice: Just continue engaging in those specifically human activities, badmouthing and backbiting.

To cheat: Change the line in midstream if it doesn't appeal to you.

Dictionary

Dictionary is an old and honored game and should be played with dignity.

Number of players: Five to eight is best; more than that can make the game too long.

Tools: A big dictionary, paper, writing implements.

To win: Get the votes of your friends.

The play: One person is designated the dictionarian for each game. He opens the book, picks a word that everyone claims is unfamiliar, spells it aloud, and writes it on a piece of paper. He also writes down the first definition given for the word, but doesn't show it to anyone. The other players write down their own definitions of the word.

There are two basic strategies: trying to approximate what the word might actually mean, and making up something outrageous — but in dictionary jargon. The definitions are handed in to the dictionarian, who numbers them in random order, along with the real one. Then each definition is read aloud by number. "Number 1, MOTMOT, any of numerous jaylike birds confined to the forests of Mexico. Number 2, MOTMOT, tasseled headgear worn by Saudi nomadic tribesmen. Number 3, MOTMOT, a small burrowing marsupial, similar to a baby anteater, whose chief habitat is the deserts of India. . . ."

Players vote for the definition they think is the real one. You get one point for guessing the true definition and one point for each vote garnered by your own definition. The dictionarian keeps a tally, announces the winner, and then reads the real definition. (Motmots are jaylike birds.)

To practice: Read the dictionary for a while to get that Webster's rhythm.

To cheat: You can cheat by knowing what the word means and not letting on. This, of course, is frowned on and won't really get you anywhere, but it's worth a try.

Related Games

Poems: A person designated as poet reads the first line of an obscure poem (a good book for this game is Stuffed Owl: An Anthology of Bad Verse) and then writes down the real second line, while everyone else makes one up. ("Farewell thou dimpled cherub Joy. . .") Proceed as in Dictionary.

Novels: Proceed as above, using the first line of a novel. ("All happy families are alike, but an unhappy family is unhappy after its own fashion, the Kinsey Institute reported today.")

Indian

A thoroughly silly game that has caused giggling in an otherwise serious round of poker.

Number of players: Two or more.

Tools: A deck of cards.

To win: Recall the law of averages and bet accordingly.

The play: The dealer shuffles the cards and passes out one card per player, face down. He decides whether the betting will be on the highest card or the lowest and announces his decision. Then, on the count of three, each player picks up his card without looking at it, licks its back, and sticks it to his forehead. Much energetic head-swiveling ensues. At any time, the dealer can call for bets. You bet as you do in poker, raising as you have the chutzpah and calling when all else is exhausted. In the case of a tie, the pot is split.

The strategy of Indian is dumb but simple. You are basically betting on statistical possibilities. If, for example, everyone in the game has low cards, you have a good chance of having a high card. If the cards are mixed, yours is probably not too distinguished either. If everyone has a high card, yours is probably low. It pays to watch people's faces very closely when the cards are first stuck in place.

To practice: The power of positive thinking can go a long way. Exercise your will-power by looking frankly full of yourself, smile contemptuously at the other players. People will begin to believe that the two on your forehead is actually an ace.

To cheat: I cheated by making a quick deal with the Roman Catholic priest sitting next to me. He assured me, by a series of winks, that my card was very high and the two of us went on to raise the betting to heady heights. In exchange, I sold my soul to God.

Zoom Schwartz Mordice

A game for those final hours when you really can't do anything at all.

Number of players: Whoever's left.

Tools: An ability to take chaos gracefully.

To win: Nobody can win, nobody can lose, we are all one with the universe.

The play: Sit in a circle. One player looks at another and says, "Zoom." Now that person has three options. She can zoom someone else, who will then zoom someone else, and so forth. Or she can respond to the person who zoomed her by saying, "Schwartz." Schwartzing has the effect of putting the initiative back in the first person's lap and can easily start a dialogue: "Zoom," "Schwartz," "Zoom," "Schwartz" . . . There is, however, the ever-present third option. The player can decide to mordice. To do this, she must look at anyone but the person who just zoomed or schwartzed her and say, "Mordice." This has exactly the same effect as schwartzing; that is, the next move is still up to the original person, but is accomplished by looking away from her.

It's your move.

Twenty Questions

A not terribly interesting game. A boring game, in fact, but because it forms the basis of so many other, more thrilling games (see Famous Last Words and Whodunit?), it is included here.

Number of players: Two or more.

Tools: Paper and pencil.

To win: Guess the secret object.

The play: One person, IT, writes down the name of some object (animate or inanimate) on a piece of paper, folds it up, and places it on a table or other highly visible place. The other players then get twenty questions (total) to find out what the object is. The questions must have a "yes" or a "no" answer. It is wise to begin with broad queries ("Is it animal?") and narrow them down as time goes on ("Is it Cary Grant?").

   The winner is the player who guesses correctly on his/her turn, and he/she gets to be the next IT.

To practice: Recall the art of deduction.

To cheat: Manage to read over IT's shoulder.

Mental Strip Poker

This game was invented by Jonathan Lipsky of Cambridge, Massachusetts.

Number of players: Enough for a good poker game.

Tools: A deck of cards.

To win: Be gutsier than the other players.

The play: Mental Strip Poker is played like a regular poker game — any version thereof — except that bets are made not with money but with the deepest, most private thoughts and fantasies of the players. To ante, for example, the dealer can demand that everyone put up one "adolescent humiliation." Once everyone's adolescent humiliation is on the table, players can raise, say, "a recent masochistic experience" or a "religious conversion" or a "bestial fantasy."

Not for the faint of heart, but the games tend to be very short.

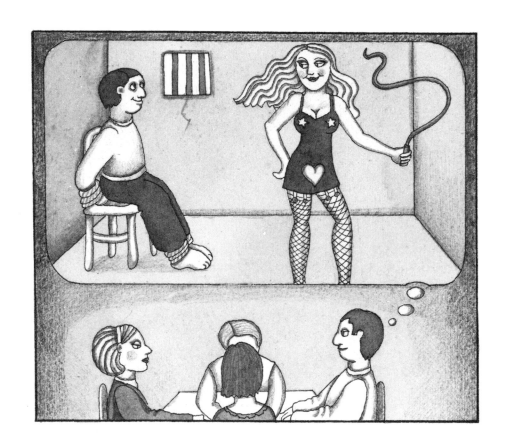

Charades

This game (pronounced charādes in this country, charădes in the other one) was so popular during the 40's and 50's that it was called "The Game." The mere mention of it can send some guests into ecstasy, others out the door. In other words, you either love Charades or you don't. But if you have never played, give it a try.

Number of players: Enough for two teams — about ten is a good number.

Tools: Paper, pencils, two hats or other bowl-shaped receptacles.

To win: Using pantomime, get your teammates to guess a phrase in less time than it takes the opposing team to guess theirs.

The play: In this game you are asked to pantomime various phrases in front of your teammates, who try vainly to guess what you're doing. You are allowed three minutes to get the phrase across.

At the outset, divide the group into two equal teams. (Among veterans the controversy starts here because they know who of their number is the best at acting or at remembering that nine verb title from the 1936 Japanese movie. It is up to the host to ensure that teams are fairly matched. One method is simply to write the names of everyone on strips of paper, stick them in the aforementioned hat, and have a blindfolded person draw them out into separate piles.)

Each team now retreats to a separate section of the house and sits down with paper and pencils to decide on the phrases which the opposing team will have to act out. You may choose from the titles of movies, plays, poems, songs, and books, plus advertising slogans and famous quotes. Because these are to be given to the enemy, you may make the phrases as impossible as you wish. It is wise to remember, however, that a truly good game rests more on creative tension than on bewildered paralysis. Much mulling should go into the decisions, much nasty rubbing together of the hands. You should come up with enough to make one for each member of the other team plus a few extra. If you want to play longer, double the number. Here are some Charades examples:

Roget's Universal Thesaurus

Passages

The Oxford Book of English Verse

"Indeed, I tremble for my country when I reflect that God is just." (Thomas Jefferson)

Tippecanoe and Tyler, too.

A Room of One's Own

The Marrakesh Express

"Like a rich jewel in an Ethiop's ear." (Romeo and Juliet)

The Greek/English Lexicon

Holocaust

Remember, the more intangible the phrase, the more difficult it is to act out.

Once you have decided on your charades, write each phrase down on a separate strip of paper. Fold the strips and place them in your hat. When both teams have filled their hats, they join each other in the parlor.

Before play actually begins, it is best to familiarize everyone with certain agreed-on shortcuts. The following gestures are used to establish the category into which the phrase falls.

Book: Palms placed together as if in prayer, then opened.

Movie: Imitate a motion picture camera by looking through a circle made by your thumb and forefinger while holding your other fist to your ear and turning your arm.

Song: Hand to open mouth, then pulled away, as if you were drawing the song from your lips.

Play: A bold gesture, right hand extended.

Poem: Draw horizontal lines with your finger.

Quote: Make quotation marks with the fingers of each hand.

After the category is established, you hold up fingers for the number of words in the phrase. Now, for the actual meat of the charade, you can use the following symbols:

First word, second word, etc.: Hold up one finger, two fingers, etc.

The: Make a "T" with your fingers.

Small word: Thumb and forefinger nearly pressed together, as "itty-bitty."

Syllable: Place fingers on forearm for number of syllables, then go to one finger on forearm for the first syllable, etc.

Past tense: Throw your hand over your shoulder.

The whole idea: Hold up your arms as if you were carrying a large globe and make waving gestures.

Start over: Hold your hands in front of you and move them back and forth, as in "Shut up."

You're close but...: Motion your teammates towards you. Or, if your team has guessed a word that is a form of your word, but yours is shorter, make a chopping motion with one hand against the palm of the other hand. Or, if they've guessed a word that is shorter than yours, move your fingers apart and together as if you were making taffy — a stretching motion.

Sounds like: Cup your hand to your ear.

Plural: Make a rolling motion with your hands.

On the nose (teammates have guessed the exact word): Place your index finger on the tip of your nose.

Once everyone feels at least acquainted with the shortcuts, you may start the game. One person is designated timekeeper, or you may trade that job back and forth. The timekeeper tosses a coin for calling. The winning team sends forth a brave soul (let's say it's you) to draw a strip from the hat. You get 30 seconds to study the title and three minutes in which to act it out.

Let us try A Room of One's Own, which is a long essay by Virginia Woolf on the rights of women (or lack of them). It is considered to be a book, so you make the signal for book. All of your teammates should respond, "BOOK." If they don't, turn them in for another team.

The title has five words in it, so hold up five fingers. Let them yell "FIVE." Then show them you're going to do the first word by holding up one finger. (An option: You can skip around in titles to do the easiest words first, as long as you let your team know what you're doing.)

Now make the itty-bitty gesture. Almost immediately, someone will yell, "A," followed by someone else who screams, "AN." Look at the "A" person and place your finger on the tip of your nose.

Now you are going to do "ROOM." Hold up two fingers, for the second word. Then show that the word has one syllable by placing one finger on your arm. Make the motion for "sounds like" and then make sweeping motions, as if you were using a broom. (Got that?) They will all cheer, "SOUNDS LIKE MOP." Just shake your head and continue until someone gets it or dead silence falls. If the latter happens, try another "sounds like." You might sit down and pretend to be a weaver — "LOOM." Or clap your hands over your ears as if you had just heard a "BOOM." After they get the "sounds like" part, look around the room you're in and make expansive gestures. You might touch all four walls. They ought to have it by now.

Now you have A ROOM. Hold up three fingers for the third word. Make the itty-bitty gesture, followed by the "sounds like" signal. Then imitate loving motions: purse your lips to kiss, cuddle your hands against your face. Okay? Did they get it? (No? Screw them.)

Now you have A ROOM OF. If you have any feminists in the group, or any persons who just happen to be well read, they should guess the whole title at this point. Let them do it. If not, go on.

Hold up four fingers for the fourth word. Signal one syllable by one finger on the forearm. Then hold up one finger and make the rolling motion for plural words. If they don't have the whole thing by now, they ought to be taught how to read. However, yours is not to educate but to dramatize, so go forward.

Hold up five fingers. Cup your hand to your ear for "sounds like." Hold an imaginary phone to your ear and then make a cutting motion. This will take forever and your time is up.

The play continues, each team taking turns until everyone has had a stab at stardom. Then the time scores are added up and the team with the least time wins.

To practice: Go to France and introduce yourself to Marcel Marceau. Barring that, take a mime class. Barring that, stand in front of your mirror and do various charades of your choice. The simplest solution is usually the best.

To cheat: Bribe a kid to read the other team's charades.

We've Got to Stop Meeting Like This

A good game for those moments when people start asking each other if they've read any good books lately. In short, a save.

Number of players: A small dinner party, more than four.

Tools: Paper and pencils for all.

To win: There are no winners in a game like this.

The play: On your sheet of paper, you write down "his name," meaning the name of someone in the room or that of a famous man or someone commonly known to the party. Fold the paper so that the name is hidden and pass it to your left. Then, beneath the fold on the paper that is handed to you, write "her name" by similar rules. Fold that over and pass to the left. Then write "where they met." Fold and pass. Then "he said." Fold and pass. Then "she said." Fold and pass. Then, taking turns, the players read aloud from the papers in their hands. For example:

Henry the Eighth met Marie Osmond at Elaine's. He said, "We've got to stop meeting like this." She said, "My dear, I just don't give a damn."

To practice: Don't.

To cheat: Peek.

Guerrilla Scrabble

Discovered by Iris M. Jarret in 1953, this is basically Scrabble minus all those tedious waits between turns.

Number of players: Two or more.

Tools: The letters from a Scrabble or Anagram game.

To win: Make more words than anyone else or steal with abandon.

The play: Sit at a table and place all the letters face down along the peripheries, leaving a fairly large hole in the middle and some space in front of each player. Then, at the word "GO," take turns turning over tiles and putting them into the center space, quickly. As the letters are brought to light, either by your hand or someone else's, keep watch for a word. (Most games start with a minimum of four-letter words.) When you see a word, shout it out and grab the letters. Place the word in front of you. Other players may then steal from you, by adding other letters to form a new word as long as the new word is not based on yours. In other words, another player could steal "cart" from you by adding "el," "cartel." But he could not add an "s" for "carts." Or a player could steal "said" and make "daisy." But he could not steal "heart" to make "heartless."

When you steal from each other, you literally steal: Take all the letters, add your own, and place them in front of you. This is important because the first person to have ten words in front of him/her wins.

Some strategy: Whenever an "s" appears on the table, grab it and add it to your words. Adding "s" makes it harder for people to steal. This is the only letter you may add to your own words.

If you are out in front, forget stealing, just make words. If you are behind, concentrate all your energies on petty thievery.

To practice: Play Scrabble into the wee hours and increase your peripheral vision by taking a lot of drugs.

To cheat: You have heard the expression, "To have an ace up your sleeve"?

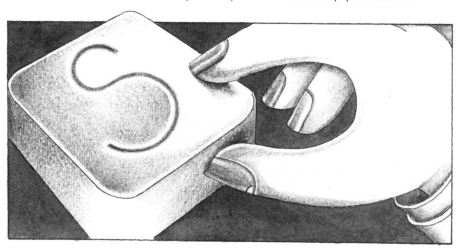

My Grandmother's Trunk

A variation on this game was played in the movie "Julia."

Number of players: Two or more.

Tools: None; quick memory is a joy forever.

To win: Remember all that has gone before you.

The play: Gather before a roaring fireplace with much cognac. The person nearest the fire begins — the play will go clockwise about the room or to each person's left. He or she says, "My grandmother's trunk has anteaters in it." The next player must say, "My grandmother's trunk has anteaters and bullfrogs in it." The next person reports, "My grandmother's trunk has anteaters, bullfrogs, and cannibals in it." The next adds, "My grandmother's trunk has anteaters, bullfrogs, cannibals, and dingbats in it." And so on until the entire alphabet is used up and the trunk is filled to brimming. And another thing: You can't laugh.

Julia's variation: This one is just a tad more complicated. One person begins by saying, "After the lion-hearted heroine bid farewell to her lover, she stood at the edge of the cliff." The next person says, "After the lion-hearted heroine bade farewell to her lover, she stood at the edge of the cliff, betraying her feelings of grief and rejection by crying out to the roaring sea." The third player adds, "After the lion-hearted heroine bade farewell to her lover, she stood at the edge of the cliff betraying her feelings of grief and rejection by crying out to the roaring sea, "Could there be another, finer face upon which his kisses fall?" And so on. Each player must repeat the entire story to date and then begin his or her line or sentence with the next letter of the alphabet.

In both versions of the game, not only must you keep a straight face, you can't pause once you've started your sentence. The loser is the first one who breaks down — usually this happens around "E."

To practice: Just do exactly what I've done here: Make up a story line by line and repeat it until you would rather do something else.

To cheat: The alphabet is a stern mistress. You can't cheat.

Categories

Brought to my attention by Doe Coover, an editor who, in her mad youth, used to spend "long liquid Sunday afternoons" playing parlor games. This is the more innocent of her two suggestions.

Number of players: Any number from two up.

Tools: Pencils and paper.

To win: Name the 19th century surgeon whose last name begins with Q.

The play: Categories is a game in which the players are asked to come up with things or people in five categories whose last names begin with a chosen five letters, all within a given time. First you must decide on the letters — any five will do — and then on the categories — a more difficult decision. You may have anything you like — Opera Stars, Celestial Bodies, Baseball Players, Novelists, Homosexual Playwrights, Gardeners, Roses, Chess Strategies, Bars, Fashion Designers, Islands, Insects, Revolutionaries, Magazines, French Chefs, Cats, Whores, Casanovas, Salads, etc. Now draw a grid of five squares across and five down — categories on top, letters down the side:

	Opera Stars	Celestial Bodies	Baseball Players	Novelists	19th Century Surgeons
J					
C					
W					
Q					
L					

Someone with a watch with a second hand times everyone — six minutes for beginners, three for pretentious snobs. When the time is up, you get a point for every box you have filled in correctly. The player with the highest score wins that round.

To practice: Pay attention next time you are around your old friend Barney with the degree in 16th century epic rhymes.

To cheat: You may, of course, make up the name of that 19th-century surgeon (Theodore M. Quark, M.D., invaluable contributions to the body of knowledge pertaining to the relationship between root canal work and psychosis). Your success depends on your dexterity.

Sexual Secrets

The guiltier of the Coover suggestions.

Number of players: Enough for a small orgy.

Tools: Please, no tools.

To win: Well. . .

The play: Or the foreplay, depending. As Coover says, "There are very few rules to the game and no real way to score (so to speak). . ." Drink a lot. Gather in a small heap. One person begins: "Tell me a sexual secret involving the number five." Everyone must reply in whatever fashion he or she can afford. ("He was five, I was sixteen." "Her five fingers explored my. . ." "'Five,' he screamed." etc.) You go on from there, taking turns, placing restrictions on the secrets as you see fit: "Tell me a sexual secret involving your mother"; "Tell me a sexual secret involving a mastiff"; "Tell me a sexual secret involving orange marmalade."

To practice: Live a fast life.

To cheat: You may lie, of course, in either direction. (You may not wish your mastiff's virtue compromised, for example, or you may not wish everyone to know that you have not been to bed with your mother.)

Wham

The trouble with this game is that you have to be able to count — quickly; thus, children tend to be better at Wham than adults.

Number of players: Two or more, preferably five to seven.

Tools: Two dice, a large strainer, corks with pieces of string strung through them, and an assortment of matches or toothpicks.

To win: Act only when the time is right.

The play: In Wham, IT attempts to entrap the corks of the other players, who, in turn, do their best to avoid the awful strainer-wham.

Before the game begins, you must string up enough corks to provide one for each guest. Using a large needle and string, run each cork right through the middle (end to end), then knot the string, leaving the cork at its end. Each string should be about a foot and a half long. Count out fifteen toothpicks or matchsticks for each player. Get out a large strainer and place the dice in it.

One person is designated IT. The others place their corks in the middle of the table, holding the other end of the string firmly in hand. IT shakes the dice in the strainer, then tosses them on the table. If the dice turn up either 7 or 11, IT must wham the strainer down on the vulnerable corks, entrapping them in its wiry cage. Each player caught must pay IT one toothpick. If all the players are caught, they must instead pay two toothpicks each.

Of course, there are other possibilities in the roll of the dice, which is where the tension comes in. If IT rolls anything other than 7 or 11, he must not wham the strainer down and the players must leave their corks in the middle — without so much as a tug on the string. This is, of course, expecting the impossible of all concerned. Now suppose that the roll of the dice yields a 6. If IT, in a moment of overanxiety, whams down the strainer, he must pay the players who have remained calm — not the ones who jerked their little corks into the safety of their laps. If, on the other hand, IT does not wham down the strainer, but several players pull their corks in, they must each pay IT a penalty of one toothpick.

Each player gets to roll the dice enough times to roll at least one seven and one eleven.

To practice: Do what everyone normally does: Spend all day throwing dice and pulling strings.

To cheat: Kick IT under the table, just as he throws the dice.

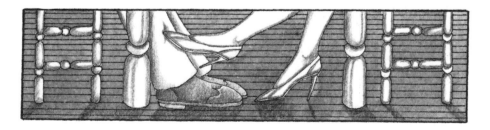

How to Increase Your Word Power

In this game, you unload all the words in your head onto a hapless scorekeeper.

Number of players: Two or more.

Tools: Paper and pen for scorekeeping.

To win: Mouth words as though they would save your life.

The play: To begin, one of the group should volunteer to be timekeeper and another to be scorekeeper. The scorekeeper arranges himself with pen and pencil and asks the group to get itself into order for play. He tells the group that each person will be given two minutes to name all the words he or she can remember that begin with a certain letter. The words must contain three or more letters; proper nouns are not allowed; only one tense of a verb and only one form of a word (singular or plural but not both) are allowed.

On the word "Go" from the timekeeper, the scorekeeper names a letter, such as "B," and begins writing down all the words the player spouts. (Don't tell players that they have goofed on any words until their time is up. The important thing about this game is not to break concentration.) At the end of two minutes, the score-keeper places his hand over the player's mouth and adds up his points — one point per allowable word.

Obviously, some beginning letters are more common than others. Thus it would not be fair, for example, to assign the first person the letter "B" and the next person the letter "X." The scorekeeper should therefore group letters into the following collections:

B, C, D, F, M, P, S, T — easy
A, G, H, I, L, R — less easy
E, N, O, U, W — hard
J, K, Q, V, X, Y, Z — hardest

The winner, naturally, is the one with the open mouth, the glazed eyes, and the highest score.

To practice: Basically, you want to stay calm. Second, once you get onto a word, ride it for all it's worth — as in "bronco, buck, boy, bust, black, beauty."

To cheat: Bribe the scorekeeper or the timekeeper or both.

Grown-up Scavenger Hunt

You remember when your mommy made up a list of little things and then you and your friends went around to houses in the neighborhood and asked the other mommies and daddies to give them to you? And Jeffrey was the one who got all the things soonest and it wasn't even his birthday? Well, this is an adult version of that game, played best by Carole Lombard in "My Man Godfrey."

Number of players: As many as your city will hold.

Tools: A list drawn up by the host(s) with copies made for as many guests as are invited, plus some extras. Moving vans are optional.

To win: Collect all the items on the list from various trusting neighbors and garbage dumps before everyone else.

The play: Because this game tends to be so long, I recommend it only as a weekend pursuit. Before anyone arrives, the master list must be drawn up. Some care should go into its preparation. These are adults, remember, well trained in the skills of moving from place to place, in persuasion and, if that fails, lying. We suggest you start with a fairly simple assortment — a Bible, for example, and a piece of letterhead stationery; a 1960 Esquire Magazine or a copy of LIFE; a half-finished bottle of Wild Turkey, a joint of good Colombian and a pair of hedge clippers. Then move onto a few more difficult items: a Yorkshire terrier, for example, an IBM Selectric, and a telephone. After those, go for the big stuff: a wingback chair, a Blackgama mink, two frozen pheasants, and an Anglican Catholic priest. Once your list is compiled, you must make sure you have enough space to accommodate several replicas of each item. And when all of your guests have arrived, hand out the lists and set a time limit. (Three hours is about right. After that it gets late and dark, not to mention the problems with the police.) The first person to complete the list, or to find the most objects within the time limit, wins. Because people tend to bring back several items at a time and then leave again, it is wise to have not too many living things on the list; also, it's good to appoint an ombudsman to watch out for the items and to tag them with not only the finder's name but the owner's name as well.

At the end of the time allotted, the hosts count up the items for each person and name the winners of first, second, and third prize. Prizes may range from silly tin whistles to bottles of champagne to estates in the country, depending on your means. Either your guests or a gang of hired teenagers should be responsible for returning the items the next day. (Don't worry, most things are insured.)

(This game can be most happily played as a charity: Owners donate used objects which are later auctioned, and players pay a playing fee.)

To practice: Bone up on rhetoric; persuasion is the key to this game. Look in the mirror and repeat, "Please give me your mink. I must win the prize so I can send my blind sister to college."

To cheat: Go out and buy everything.

Whales Tails

A drinking game from the Ivy League.

Number of players: Five or more.

Tools: Alcohol in large quantities.

To win: Be the last to fall down.

The play: Gather in a circle. One person is designated IT or Zero. From Zero's left the other players count off around the circle. Then Zero says, "The Prince of Wales lost his tail. Whales tails. Seven, sir (or Fifteen or Two or whatever)." Now Seven must immediately respond, "Nay, sir." Then Zero asks, "Who, sir?" Seven says, "Eight, sir." (Or Nine or Four or whatever.) At this point, the accused (Seven) has become Zero and everyone else must quickly recount to find himself. Specifically, if Seven is now Zero, Eight is not sitting just next to him, but is actually eight persons away. The new Eight must immediately respond, "Nay, sir," and so the game continues. Any pause or mistake is cause for penalty. In the charming Ivy League colleges, penalties are exacted by requiring that the person take a drink, although the game goes right on. In more civilized settings, people who lose count are allowed to fall asleep.

To practice: Just repeat after me, "One, two, three. . ."

To cheat: Water your whiskey.

Murder #1

Murder is a game for people who have not outgrown a good scare.

Number of players: Any number up to 52.

Tools: A deck of cards, no jokers.

To win: The murderer wins by killing everybody else; anyone else can win by escaping death and catching the killer.

The play: Deal one card to each player, being sure to include the ace of spades. Sit in a circle and pass out the cards, face down, one to each person. Each player looks at his card and keeps what he sees to himself. The player with the ace of spades is the murderer. Now, sit for a little while and smile at each other. Murderer ready? Okay, the way you kill people is by winking at them. One eye, very fast. Victims ready? If someone winks at you — one eye, very fast — wait exactly ten seconds (count to ten silently) and then say, "I'm dead." You are now permanently out of the game.

To catch the killer, you must be quick. If you see someone wink at someone else, immediately say to the intended victim, "Are you dead?" If she answers, "Yes," you may name your suspect. If the guess is right, the murderer must give himself up. If it is wrong, the game simply goes on. There are no penalties, curiously, either for queries or accusations. That means, of course, that the murderer can make them as well, just to confuse things.

To practice: Good winkers are hard to find. The wink must be very, very swift. Time spent in front of a mirror will pay off.

To cheat: One way to cheat is to make a lot of death queries when you are the murderer. People will begin to suspect you, however, if you are wrong for the tenth time. I also remember a game in which someone figured out who the murderer was and kept winking at her, which so unnerved the culprit that she botched her next job.

Murder #2

I am indebted to Gilbert Johnson of Venice, California, who wrote me a letter accusing me of "perverting the perfectly legitimate parlor game of Murder into a childish winking contest" after he read the aforementioned account in a magazine. I apologize, Mr. Johnson. Here is your version.

Number of players: Ideally, seven to fifteen.

Tools: A big house or any place where hide-and-seek can be played. Also, a deck of cards.

To win: The murderer wins by killing everyone else or by eluding detection by the investigator. The investigator wins by catching the murderer. The others win by not being killed.

The play: Cards, including the king of hearts and the ace of spades, are dealt to each player. The person who draws the king of hearts declares himself the investigator and retreats to a small, secluded room; a bathroom does very nicely. The other players pocket their cards and mingle or hide. The murderer, of course, is the one with the ace of spades. He or she kills people by touching them gently on the shoulder and saying, "You're dead." The victim must then fall to the ground if standing, or freeze if prone. (Mr. Johnson was once killed on a roof and had to dangle his foot over the edge to signal his demise.) The play continues until the murderer slaughters everyone or until another player, upon finding a victim, rushes to inform the investigator. The investigator then lines up the living, including the murderer, and questions them ("Where were you when the body was found?" "Who did you see near the body?") Everyone except the murderer must tell the truth. The investigator gets one chance to name the suspect.

To practice: Murderers should learn how to win the confidence of innocent people and how to kill quickly. Investigators should read Sherlock Holmes and watch reruns of Perry Mason. Victims should practice falling gracefully.

To cheat: Given the proper (?) incentives, innocents have been known to provide the murderer with an alibi by lying, too. This is, of course, against the rules. However, certain favors can be bought by this method, having to do with other, more pleasurable games.

Murder #3

There is, believe it or not, yet another version of this dreadful pastime. It begins exactly like Mr. Johnson's game: the players draw cards, and investigator declares himself and retreats. However, the remaining players do not leave the room; they turn off the lights and get down on all fours. Then everyone, including the murderer, commences crawling around on the floor.

The murderer kills in the same way as before, by brushing the shoulder and saying, "You're dead." The victim then falls the relatively short distance to the floor. Innocents discover victims by bumping into them and they alert the investigator by crawling to the bathroom (never has this phrase been taken so literally). Once alerted, the investigator rushes into the room and turns on the lights. As the lights go on, everyone must freeze. (This is not, therefore, the wisest game in which to start that intimate liaison.) The investigator then pokes about the bodies and questions the living, still frozen in position, until he names a suspect. "Truth will come to light; murder cannot be hid long."*

*William Shakespeare, The Merchant of Venice, Act. II, Sc. 2, L. 86.

Alibi

A game based on the premise that you can't resist the truth.

Number of players: Four or more.

Tools: A deck of cards and a criminal mind.

To win: The suspects win by being more convincing than the next guy. The inspector wins by fingering the one who did it.

The play: As in the various versions of Murder, count out as many cards as there are players, making sure that the queen of hearts and the ace of spades are included. Then shuffle the cards and deal them out. The player who draws the queen of hearts is the inspector. The one who draws the ace of spades is the killer and keeps it to himself.

The inspector steps forward and announces that she has just found Sir Cloudsley Shovel in the swimming pool (or basement or attic or whatever) and that Sir Shovel was killed around 10:00 (or whenever). She lines everyone up and asks them, please, to answer "a few questions." In this game, a turnabout from Murder #2, all the other suspects are making up whatever stories they like, but the killer must include the truth in his story. In fact, he must manage to tell the inspector that he did the deed and how — but he must disguise this truth in the telling.

Suspect 1 begins by saying that he was not near the swimming pool the whole day, but was sketching in the drawing room. However, he whispers, near 10:00 he saw Suspect 2 running past the rose bushes outside his window.

Suspect 2 must then explain her behavior. She was, for example, merely practicing her soccer game. However, she did see Suspect 3 peering down at the pool from his bedroom.

Suspect 3 explains: "I was only trying to remember a line from Yeats" and adds, "but I saw Suspect 4 climbing out of the pool with a pair of hedge clippers."

Suspect 4 explains that he fell into the pool while cutting roses for afternoon tea but that just before he fell in, he saw Suspect 5 wiping her hands of blood in the Jacuzzi near the pool edge.

Suspect 5 explains that the "blood" was actually red paint from the gazebo she was painting and that she wanted to get it off her hands quickly because she had a luncheon date. However, she saw Suspect 1 with a snorkel in the drawing room shortly after the time of the demise.

Suspect 1 replies that he was merely checking out his scuba equipment.

It is up to the inspector to sift through this data and single out one suspect as the guilty one. She may ask one question of each individual and must keep in mind that while everyone else is simply reacting to the accusation of a fellow suspect, the killer is both explaining his behavior and bragging of his dreadful deed. (This, naturally, makes things rather difficult for the killer because he has no idea where he was seen or what he was doing until the suspect before him starts singing. He must, therefore, explain away the story of his comrade while dropping a well-disguised hint to the inspector — killers always like someone to know they did it.)

The inspector, in this case, is quite perceptive and her first question is addressed to Suspect 3: "What was the line from Yeats you were trying to recall?" Suspect 3 growls:

> The blood-dimmed tide is loosed, and everywhere,
> The ceremony of innocence is drowned.

The inspector immediately accuses Suspect 3 of having killed Sir Shovel by stabbing, then rolling him into the pool. Suspect 3 sheepishly shows the ace and is dragged off in chains.

The game, as you may well have gathered, can get very surreal since only one person, the killer, knows what's going on. And he must fit his story into those of the others. This is made more difficult by the aforementioned fact that the killer has no idea what the person before him is going to say. It is wise, therefore, to allow about five minutes before the questioning begins for the suspects to "consider their situations" at the time of the crime. This gives the killer time to decide how he murdered someone. Brief pauses before questions are allowable and, if you want to make the game interesting, it behooves everyone to behave in as guilty a manner as is possible.

If the inspector's guess is correct, she may take another turn at playing detective or the cards may be shuffled and dealt out again. If the killer gets away with his crime, he becomes the next inspector.

To practice: Listen hard. Imagine well. If you intend to be a killer, think of "blanket alibis" that should fit, no matter what the accusation.

To cheat: Whatever you do, the truth will out.

59

Adverbs

A game played most winsomely in "Hay Fever," a play by Noel Coward in which four houseguests get more than they bargained for.

Number of players: More than three, about eight to fifteen is best.

Tools: Various living room objects.

To win: Guess the operative adverb.

The play: One person is IT and leaves the room. The others must come up with an adverb which they feel they can personify because, when IT returns, she will demand that they do various acts "in the manner of the word." Thus the word should not be too easy or too hard, but somehow, as Goldilocks says, "just right." Expect much discussion and disagreement, not to mention outright belligerency. Once the matter is settled, call IT back into the room.

IT may begin by saying to anyone, for example, "So-and-so, go give a drink to What's-his-name, in the manner of the word." Let us say the word is "saucily." Thus, So-and-so rises and, with a long sideways glance, sidles over to the bar. He lifts a bourbon and, clasping it to his chest, sidesteps over to What's-his-name, chucks him under the chin, and hands it over. If the word were "intensely," So-and-so would march to the bar, capture the bourbon, and after staring into its depths, stride over to What's-his-name and, kissing him on both cheeks, hand it over. IT may ask anyone to do anything "in the manner of the word"; only the law and compassion stand in her way. She continues until her victims are exhausted or she guesses the word. The last actor becomes the next IT.

Some suggested words:
lavishly
doggedly
secretly
amicably
sociably
illegally
accusingly
reproachfully
freely
wildly
malevolently
caressingly
vauntingly
modestly
wonderfully

To practice: Read the lists of adverbs in Roget's Thesaurus and give your imagination free rein.

To cheat: IT may hire a confederate who will, by a prearranged signal system, let him know what the adverb is. More trouble than it's worth.

Marienbad

Also called Nim; played in the film "Last Year at Marienbad."

Number of players: Two.

Tools: Sixteen pennies.

To win: Leave your opponent holding the penny.

The play: Arrange the pennies in a four-row triangle: one penny on top, three in the next row, then five, and finally seven. Take turns removing pennies — as few as one or as many as a whole row — but from only one row at a time. The game continues until one person is left with the last penny. There is a mathematical solution to Marienbad, which everyone has forgotten.

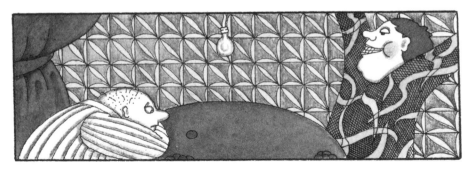

Spoon

This ridiculous game was brought to my attention by Janet Huseby, who met her husband, Bob Smith, over a spoon table. She loathed him on that occasion, because he never failed to say "Little Chester." After you have played, you will see what I mean. . . .

Number of players: Three to thirteen.

Tools: A deck of cards and an assortment of old spoons.

To win: Gather four cards of a kind, grab a spoon, and be careful who you talk to.

The play: There are two parts to Spoon; Part II is more ludicrous than Part I. In Part I, you try to gather four cards of a kind (four threes, for example) and then grab a spoon. In Part II, you continue trying to gather four cards of a kind and to grab a spoon, and meanwhile you also try to get people who aren't supposed to talk to you to do so or you try to avoid talking to people you're not supposed to, or both. Ready?

First, with the cards face up, count out four of a kind in as many values as there are players. For example, if there are five players, you might count out four aces, four kings, four nines, four sixes, and four threes. Put the rest of the cards away. Then count out enough spoons to equal the number of people, minus one, and place the spoons either in the center of the table or underneath it, business ends facing the middle.

One person is designated dealer. (On subsequent rounds, it moves to the right or to the left, who cares?) He shuffles the cards and deals them out until everyone has four cards and there are no cards left. The dealer then says "One, two, three, pass!" and everyone, with great speed, passes one card to the right. Card-passing continues, with gathering urgency, until someone gets four of a kind. He then grabs a spoon, a gesture which can be compared to dropping the flag at Indy, because once someone has gone for a spoon, everyone must go for the spoons.

The term "going for the spoons" should be clarified at this point. Veteran Spoon players do not, if the spoons are on top of the table, simply reach over and pick up a spoon. No. First they make a motion toward the spoons like that of a particularly nasty king cobra toward a stupid mongoose; once they have annexed the spoon to their fingers, they then, by accident of course, smash all the other spoons with their fist, spraying them into all corners of the room, causing the other players to leap to their feet, knock over their chairs, sprain their ankles, and generally behave like so many bewildered baboons whose only purpose in life has suddenly become to find that spoon and hold onto it. To cause this havoc is, of course, a great deal of fun even if it is totally against the rules.

The card game and the resulting melee form the core of Spoon. However, there is a second part, a sort of overlay to the first. As card-passing resumes, the loser of round one — the player who didn't get a spoon — becomes a Pig One, one of nine possible ratings. These are in order of social standing, Pigs One, Two, and Three; Sows One, Two and Three; and Hogs One, Two, and Three. (Please do not ask how these classifications came to be.) The first time you lose a round, you

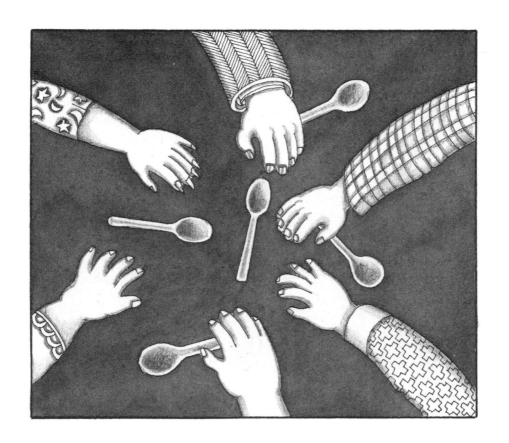

become a Pig One. If you lose again, you become a Pig Two, and so on down the line until you are a Hog Three and not only disreputable but out of the game. Got that?

There is, however, another way to become a Pig or Sow or Hog. Part II of Spoon is a lesson in class warfare, because while people of the lower classes can speak to each other and to people of the upper classes, people from the upper classes cannot speak to them. That is, you can always talk to someone above you in the social order, but you cannot talk to anyone below you. Hogs, for example, may speak to anyone (there is no distinction, for this purpose, within classifications — Hogs One and Two are the same Hog); Sows may speak to other Sows and to Pigs, but not to Hogs; Pigs may speak to other Pigs, and to those who are not, as yet, classified, but not to Sows or Hogs. Unclassified people speak only to each other (which is the way it is in the upper classes).

Now, here is the rub: If someone from an upper class makes the mistake of speaking to someone from a lower class, he or she instantly becomes a member of that lower class. If, for example, a Sow talks to a Hog, she becomes a Hog One; if an unclassified person speaks to a Pig, he become a Pig One; and so on. (You become a "one" no matter what the number of the person speaking to you; it's the category that counts.) And so, most of Part II of Spoon consists of Pigs, Hogs, and Sows trying in all manner of sly and suggestive ways to get people of unsullied virtue to talk to them. They do it casually, "Say, Bob, is it your deal or mine?"; dramatically, "Susan, your dress is on fire."; indecently and at every opportunity, "Bob? Susan? Didn't I see you two together the other night at that cheap motel?"

66

and there is only one way to protect your purity from these swine. You must exercise the last resort of gentlepersons, "Little Chester."

If, for example, a Hog turns to you and says, "May I have a cigarette?" you respond by looking up at the ceiling and saying, "Little Chester, yes you may." As long as you precede your sentence with "Little Chester," you may respond in any way you like. There is some argument as to whether or not you should look at the person while saying "Little Chester"; I think it wise to look at the ceiling.

All of these conversations, it should be remembered, are going on while the players are still furiously playing round after round of cards, trying to get four of a kind, grabbing spoons, and dashing all over the room. Good luck.

To practice: You should practice eye-hand coordination, spoon-grabbing techniques, and sprinting. (The study of spoon-grabbing is best accomplished by buying several small children one bowl of chocolate pudding.) As for mastering the art of saying "Little Chester," that is a talent one is born with — it is rarely acquired. In general, it takes a personality obsessed with the insignificant things in life. However, if you must, you may practice the art in your responses to people who talk to you throughout the day: "Little Chester, thank you for taking me to lunch"; "Little Chester, you're standing on my foot"; "Little Chester, your place or mine?" This may earn you a short detainment in one of our mental facilities, but the resulting expertise will be worth it.

Paper Bag

A game of illusion and disguises.

Number of players: Enough for two teams or more — four to twenty.

Tools: Paper bags, prepared by the hosts, filled with goodies as described below.

To win: Be voted the best in the senior play.

The play: Before the guests arrive, fill a number of bags with props that can be used to form the basis for short skits. In one, for example, you might place a pair of sunglasses, a pencil, a small ceramic frog, two cubes of sugar, and a dimestore ring; in another, a map, a lampshade, a bottle of Windex, and a business card. The more various and incompatible the assortment, the better.

Once the guests have settled in, have them divide into teams. Hand a bag to one of the teams and give the team ten minutes to make up a pantomime skit based on the contents of the bag. The skit must last no more than, say, 20 minutes, and every item in the bag must be used, hopefully to its fullest advantage.

Using the first bag's contents, the team might come up with the following skit: A man wearing sunglasses comes onto the "stage," takes the pair of sugar cubes out of his pocket, and begins throwing them onto a nearby table top, picking them up, shaking them in his fist, and throwing them again. A woman walks in and sits down. Our hero eyes her carefully. She ignores him. At this point, another man rushes into the "bar," brandishing the ceramic frog and heading straight for our hero. He reaches for whatever's handy, finds the pencil in his pocket, and holds it out in front of him. Stunned, the man halts in mid-lunge. The woman claps appreciatively, then walks over to the frog man and, taking his arm, begins to walk out with him. He waves his hand in farewell, showing off his diamond ring. Our hero, dejected, goes back to his "dice." Another member of the team rushes onto the stage carrying a sign which reads, "The pen may be mightier than the toad, but diamonds are a girl's best friend."

And so on. The teams take turns as long as the bags hold out. The only rules are that you must use everything in the bag and the skits can't run over the time limit. When all teams have completed their skits, take a vote on the winning team.

To practice: Take a few things from your desk drawer and make up a story about them.

To cheat: To cheat is a sin against the imagination.

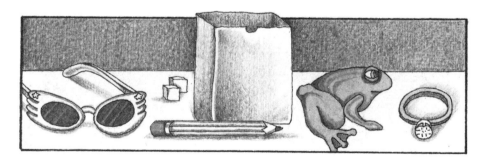

Proverbs

A wonderful game for wet afternoons in Manhattan when you don't want to go to the museum and you don't like the movies in town.

Number of players: More than two — about ten is good.

Tools: A head for Benjamin Franklin; an ear for the right word.

To win: Guess the proverb from the clues given.

The play: One person is chosen as IT and leaves the room. The others decide on a proverb appropriate for the occasion. Keep in mind that when IT returns, he will begin asking questions of each player, going clockwise around the room. The first player must include the first word of the proverb in his answer, the second player must use the second, and so on until the proverb is complete. IT can ask any question he wants, except, of course, "What is the proverb?"

Let us say the players decide on "Let sleeping dogs lie." Call IT back into the room. Tell him that the proverb has four words. He asks the first player, "How is the weather?" The player responds, "Let me think; the weather is hot and musty." (This player is obviously an expert, for she has thrown a red herring to IT by the use of the word "musty." This will lead him to think that the proverb is, "Musty is as musty does.")

IT asks the second player, "And how do you think the weather is?" (Now, IT has been shown to be familiar with "Proverbs" as well, for he appears to be using the proverbial tack of addressing the same question to each person.) The second player responds, "Weather for dancing, weather for eating, weather for sleeping, weather for loving." Very good, second player. An excellent job of camouflage.

IT addresses the third player, "Weather?" And the third player answers: "Dog day afternoon," nearly undoing the handiwork of his friends.

The fourth responds to the question with, "The kind of weather to lie around in."

If IT hasn't gotten the proverb by now, you may engage in a second round. IT should be reminded of the length of the proverb at this point so that he doesn't get hopelessly confused. You may go through it a third time, and if IT doesn't get the proverb then, retire him.

Some suggestions for proverbs to try are:

A bird in the hand is worth two in the bush.

Don't count your chickens before they hatch.

Honesty is the best policy.

If wishes were horses, beggars would ride.

Don't cry over spilt milk.

Forewarned is forearmed.

All's fair in love and war.

A fool and his money are soon parted.

A penny saved is a penny earned.

A friend in need is a friend indeed.

A rolling stone gathers no moss.

Early to bed and early to rise makes a man healthy, wealthy and wise.

To practice: Memorize proverbs, then go around throwing pieces of them into sentences. Make sure you can keep a straight face.

To cheat: IT may cheat by putting his ear to the door.

Five-Way Tick-Tack-Toe or Go-Muko

Very simple and surprisingly challenging, the invention of John Freeman, a mad gamesman.

Number of players: Two.

Tools: A piece of graph paper and two pencils.

To win: Get five X's or five O's in a row.

The play: Place the graph paper between the two players, one of whom is X and the other O. The players take turns marking the squares. The first person to get five in a row — vertically, horizontally, or diagonally — wins. Be aware that the alternate title of this game contains the word "Go"; anyone who has played "Go" knows that it looks simple and is actually almost impossible.

To practice: Play "Go."

To cheat: You can't.

Going Blank

A game in which you will discover yourself to have an IQ of 33, the memory of a banana, and the reflexes of an armchair.

Number of players: A lot, ten to twenty.

Tools: Nothing will help.

To win: Keep track of everything everyone has said and stay on your toes.

The play: One person, IT, chooses three categories of anything under the sun. Let us say she chooses Birds, Comedians, and Churches. (She might just as well have chosen Rocks, Popes, 18th-century Novels, Baseball Teams, Fruits, Chemicals, Poets, or Criminals. . .) Okay? When IT points at you and says, "Churches," you answer, "St. Patrick's" (or whatever) within ten seconds or you're out of the game. You may choose churches of the burg in which you're playing or famous churches, as long as they are known to the rest of the players — no fair making up a chapel on the hill of your home town. (See "To cheat") Next IT points to someone across the room and pronounces, "Flowers." "Wisteria" the victim answers. Then IT comes back to you and yells, "Churches" and you say, "Mother of God," which does not count.

IT must keep moving her finger about the room like some sort of lightning rod. She should hit people with the same category several times unless it is obvious that they studied Gothic architecture in high school, in which case she should ask them about flowers. The last person to go out is the next IT.

You will be amazed at how dumb you are.

To practice: Watch daytime game shows.

To cheat: Make up outrageous answers and challenge anyone who challenges you to a fistfight.

Pruie

A good game for people who have become bored with the finer things in life.

Number of players: A cocktail crowd is good, four or more.

Tools: A good ear.

To win: Find the Pruie.

The play: Once the crowd is gathered, the host secretly designates someone as the Pruie — you can do this with playing cards. Then the players close their eyes and begin walking around the room. Whenever you bump into someone, which you undoubtedly will, you say, "Pruie?" to which the proper response is "Pruie." If, however, you bump into the real Pruie, he or she should respond by remaining silent. So, if you bump into a person who remains silent when you say "Pruie?", you know you have done it. You have found the Pruie. You may then open your eyes and stand near the Pruie. The last one to find the Pruie is the guy wandering around alone with his eyes closed.

As the Pruie, your duty is serious. You may keep your eyes open the whole time and avoid bumping people. However, you may not go to great lengths, like leaving the room, only short lengths, like climbing the nearest chair when a person bears down on you. The Pruie gets the fun of seeing all those people bashing each other around the room.

A Related Game

Vampire: Someone, as in Pruie, is designated the Vampire. In this game, everyone, even the Vampire, must keep his or her eyes closed. The Vampire sneaks around the room, placing his or her hands around the other players' throats. If the Vampire strangles you, you must let out a bloodcurdling scream. Once you are strangled, then you, too, are a Vampire and you, too, strangle people. Lest you think that's all there is to this macabre game, there is a wrinkle. If two Vampires strangle each other, then they cancel out the essence of Vampire, so to speak, and become mortal again, thus keeping the victim supply fresh. As you may have guessed, this game can go on indefinitely.

To practice: Don't.

To cheat: Cheating is about the same for both games. In Pruie, you can pretend to be the Pruie when you're not or, if you are the Pruie, you can pretend not to be. In Vampire, you can pretend to be a Vampire or you can pretend you're not. I am not sure why you would want to do this, but it takes all kinds.

Whodunit?

The title is a slight misnomer, for a more apt description would be "How was it done?" These are puzzles, really, most of them involving dead bodies.

Number of players: Two or more.

Tools: None. A methodical mind may or may not help.

To win: Guess how or why it was done.

The play: One player describes the scene of the crime or the particular puzzlement. The others engage in Twenty Questions until they determine what happened, keeping in mind that each tableau contains a major clue as well as efforts to disguise it. Once you've got the hang of them, you can make them up yourself. For example:

Mary was lying dead on the floor surrounded by water and broken glass. The window was open and the curtains blew ominously in the wind. Who done it?

The man lay face down in the desert sand. He had a pack on his back and his boot laces were loose. It was hot. He was dead. Who done it?

A man who lives on the 20th floor goes to work in the morning. He gets into the elevator and pushes the button for One. In the evening he comes home, gets in the elevator and pushes the button for Ten. Then he walks the rest of the way up. Why?

Answers are given on page 110.

Famous Last Words

This game was invented by Mary K. Pratt of Long Beach, California.

Number of players: Two or more.

Tools: Nothing special; a fondness for funeral parlor gossip will help.

To win: Guess the name of a famous person, most definitely dead.

The play: One person is designated IT. That person thinks up a famous person, fictional or real, and either recalls or imagines what that person's last words were or might have been. While the other players gather in respectful silence, IT utters those words. Any player may guess the hidden identity immediately, but each player is allowed only one guess. If the name is not guessed at once, the players must engage in a form of Twenty Questions, plying IT with "yes" or "no" questions about the gender, occupation, age of his/her famous person. The person who wins becomes the next IT and so on. Some examples:

Abraham Lincoln: "I hope the second act is better."

Jesse James (who was shot in the back while hanging a picture): "Is it straight yet?"

Scarlett O'Hara: "I'll think about all of it tomorrow, at Tara."

To practice: Skim Bartlett's Familiar Quotations. It will not give you too many actual last words, but will remind you of how people speak when in a serious situation.

To cheat: You can't.

Decadence

One of the more nasty parlor games.

Number of players: Three or more, preferably more.

Tools: None.

To win: Understand that you can't win.

The play: Some poor soul is sent from the room with the understanding that while he's away the others will make up a narrative which he must uncover by questions that can be answered only "yes," "no," or "maybe."

This, of course, is hard. Really hard. Finding a noun by getting "yes," "no," or "maybe" answers is one thing — but finding a whole story? Yech! Well, it's made even harder by the fact that while the victim is out of the room, the other players don't make up a story at all. Instead they agree to let the last word in each question determine the answer — "yes" if that word ends in a consonant, "no" if it ends in a vowel, and "maybe" if it ends with the letter "y."

When IT returns, he can begin by asking "Does the story have a plot?" "Yes," replies the first player. "Does it have a heroine?" "No," replies the second player. "Does it have a hero who is black?" "Yes," replies the third player. And so on. (A famous example of this game can be found in Spectorsky's The Exurbanites, in which he describes the bildungsroman of a young midget who is raped by a locomotive.) After 15 minutes or so, either the person guesses what's going on or the group tells him. When it's all over, you can tell the chagrined victim that he made the whole story up himself, as my friend Mr. O'Keefe says, "out of his sick unconscious mind."

To practice: Don't.

To cheat: IT may cheat by knowing the trick — and thus, self-consciously, making up a story out of his sick unconscious mind.

Ghost

Ghost is a word game, often played in cars on dumb trips.

Number of players: Two or more.

Tools: Spelling ability.

To win: Do not be the first to spell GHOST.

The play: In each round the players take turns naming letters which will, eventually, add up to a word. The point is not to be the poor slob who completes the word. Each time you are, you will be given one more letter in the word GHOST. The first person to spell GHOST is the loser.

One person, it does not matter who, begins by saying a letter, any old letter will do. Let us try "T." The next person adds a letter to the first one, say "R." Then the next person — or the original player in the case of just two — adds a third letter, say "A." So far we have TRA, right? Okay. Now the next person is in some danger because it is here, on the fourth letter, that things get rough. The point is not to add a letter that will result in a word. So let us say you add "I." A nice letter, an innocuous letter, nothing wrong with the letter "I." However, in this case, it puts the next person in line in a very awkward position. How is he or she going to avoid that tempting, that luscious, that beckoning, that — dare we say it — "N"? And thereby spell the Cannonball that spells disaster? By adding a "P," that's how! TRAIP! Oh glorious TRAIP! (Not so glorious in a two-person game, though — read on.) The next person can safely say "S." But now to TRAIPS, one can add only "E" or "ING." Whichever way it goes, the last person gets the "G" of GHOST and a new round begins.

By this time, dear reader, you have gathered that this seemingly dull wallflower of a game is actually a siren in disguise, requiring the foresight and cunning of a chessmaster. The tension in a room full of Ghost players could be made into drapes and hung at Westminster.

A couple of rules to remember: There is no penalty for spelling a word on the third letter — that happens too often for it to be fair to fine the poor third party. It is at the fourth letter that things begin to count.

(2) Everyone must, all along, be building toward some real word, without completing it. In other words, you can't throw in a "Z" after TRAI; that ruins the game, not to mention spoiling someone's winning strategy.

(3) Scrabble rules apply in deciding what words are allowable. You may accuse players of having completed words when they claim they have not, but if you are wrong, you will be penalized one letter of the word GHOST.

Remember: This game is treacherous; play very carefully.

To practice: Bone up on mono- and polysyllables.

To cheat: You can accuse others of having spelled a word when, in actuality, they have not. But you should remember, it's your neck.

Long Division

A numbers game for the logically inclined.

Number of players: One.

Tools: The problem below and a pencil.

To win: Fill in the missing numbers.

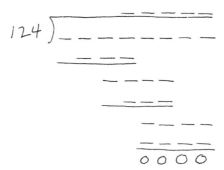

A couple of hints: (1) Notice that the problem comes out even. (2) You do not have to start at the beginning. The answer is given on pages 110–111.

Six Characters

This is not really a game, but is included for its psychological instruction. It is limited to seven players only.

One person sits down and decides which six people — actual, fictional, living, or dead — have had the most influence on his life, who meant or means the most. It is good to try for three men and three women. Once she's got them, she assigns one character to each person in the room, then sits back and listens to them talk. (One friend had Marilyn Monroe, Jean Arthur, Hamlet, Hannah Arendt, Nietzsche, and Muhammed Ali.)

The conversation is interesting for the person who thinks up the characters because they are, essentially, different aspects of her character. It can be very unnerving as well.

The Scissors Game

A game of such subtlety that only the very lucky can figure it out.

Number of players: Enough for a nice circle of people — six or more.

Tools: A pair of scissors.

To win: Guess the secret of the crossed (or uncrossed) blades.

The play: The secret of this game is a particularly nasty little twist. In the game, you are asked to tell a single line of a continuing story and then pass the scissors to the next person, saying as you do so, "crossed" or "uncrossed." People who don't know the secret will assume that you mean the scissor blades (open or closed) when, in fact, you do not. You mean your ankles or your legs. A typical game is described below.

It is best if about half the people playing know the secret. Usually this happens as a matter of course, but if your group has been particularly isolated from the parlor, have someone on the inside initiate at least three other people. Then sit down in a neat circle (it is very important that you sit in a circle) and one person (who knows the secret) explains that in this game each person will tell a line or two of a story and then pass the scissors to the next person, who will continue the story and pass on the scissors, etc.

The first person picks up the scissors and says, for example, "The other day upon the stair I met a man who wasn't there." Then she passes the scissors to her right,

saying as she passes them, "And now I pass the scissors to X, uncrossed." The blades on the scissors are closed. The next person, who should also know the secret, says, "He wasn't there again today" (or some such) and passes the scissors to his right, saying, "And now I pass the scissors to Y, uncrossed." This time the blades are open, or crossed. Depending on Y's attentiveness, he or she may or may not notice something amiss. But there is generally someone who does and who begs exception. "Ahem," he or she will say, "The scissor blades appear to be crossed." And then she or he will sit back and smile. The person who is passing the scissors should look at him or her with great contempt and pass the scissors again, saying, "uncrossed." Y, the person accepting the scissors, is by now in a state of bewilderment; the person who first noticed this arrogant abuse of the rules is rapidly getting furious.

This may go on for some time until Y insists on accepting the scissors and getting on with the game. She says something like, "My God I wish he'd go away" and passes the scissors with the blades closed, saying, "I pass the scissors to W, uncrossed." (And thinking to herself that this is a boring game.) Unfortunately, the first player points out to Y that she has passed the scissors incorrectly and must do it again. This shocks Y, who argues that the blades are closed and she has said "uncrossed." "Too bad," retorts the first player, "It's wrong." The player who before noticed the discrepancy between blades and speech jumps in demanding satisfaction. Y, in an effort to please, tries passing the scissors open, saying "uncrossed" and is told, once again, that she has not met the challenge. Y, near tears, happens to glance down at the legs of the players in front of her. Light dawns. She adjusts her legs and passes the scissors to the next player with the blades closed once again and says, "uncrossed." "Very good," responds the first player. Our attentive player is now in a towering rage. "How could this be?" he demands. The knowing ones smile.

The play may go on for quite some time before it becomes obvious that there is no relation between the scissor blades and "crossed" or "uncrossed." Players nervous about the shape of the universe will attempt to force a relationship and will be shot down. Cynical players will pass the scissors nonchalantly, blades crossed, uncrossed, whatever, and will mutter "crossed" or "uncrossed" depending on their mood. They, too, will be shot down, much to their surprise. There is a relationship here, as you know, but it lies in the knees and the ankles, not in the blades.

How soon you tell the in-the-dark players the secret of the scissors rests on Christian charity. Some of them will guess right off, others will remain ignorant forever. This phenomenon appears to be unrelated to brains or breeding, but lies instead in the realm of the open mind.

To practice: You should practice telling a story, crossing and uncrossing your legs and passing scissors in one motion.

To cheat: I can't imagine how you would cheat.

Hinkie Pinkie

Another good game for dumb car trips.

Number of players: Two or more.

Tools: None.

To win: Be funnier than the next guy.

The play: After the first 6000 miles, turn to your driving companions and say, "What's a white man's mule called?" They will look baffled, not to say dumbfounded, not to say dazed; you reply, "A honky donkey."

Then it's someone else's turn. He or she could say, "What're existential twin cows called?" Answer: "Moomoo Camus." (That's disgusting.) A fantasy cleaner? A wishy washy.

You can also play Hink Pink. What is a rich politician? A fat cat. What's an immoral bird? A loose goose, etc.

Then there's Hinkity Pinkity. What's an ambiguous pope? A wait-and-see papacy, etc.

A Related Game

What Kind of Animal?: This game was invented by the editor of this book, Ann Dilworth, which should give you an idea of the burdens writers must suffer.

The number of players and so forth are the same as above. The first player says, "In the forest I met a dear deer who said he saw a _____." Her companion replies, "A bare bear." Or a "new gnu." "A hoarse horse." Now you think of one. Remember, the adjective must sound exactly like the noun. (That's called a homonym.)

The "Singin' in the Rain" Game

A game based on musicals, in which everyone gets to imagine that he or she is Gene Kelly.

Number of players: Enough for two teams.

Tools: A piano or other musical instrument is helpful, but not mandatory.

To win: Arrange to have Betty Comdon and Adolph Green on your team.

The play: Players are asked to remember song lyrics from famous musicals or, if they can't, to fake them without getting caught.

Divide into two teams, then sit across from each other, knee to knee. The first person on one team begins by starting to sing a song from a well-loved musical: "I'm singin' in the rain, just. . ." Here he stops abruptly. The person sitting across from him must pick up the lyric without missing a beat, "Singin' in the rain, what a glorious feeling, I'm. . ." Here she stops. The player opposite her sings, "Happy again." Now the next person has no idea what follows this phrase, but he does remember the tune, thank God, so he makes up a line: "The clouds up above. . ." Now the odds are good to fair that he will get away with it because (a) no one on his own team is going to turn him in and (b) the only person who can actually call him on it is the opposite player, who is usually too nervous to notice. Unfortunately, in this case the opposite player is Adolph Green (the author of "Singin' in the Rain"). The way Mr. Green announces that he has caught the impostor is by changing the song in midstream. He sings, "New York, New York, it's a wonderful town!" The player who tried and failed is now out of the game (he becomes the audience). The rest of the players continue with the new song until someone else runs out of lyrics, in which case she, too, tries to fool her opposite number. If she's successful, the show just goes on.

The team with the last player left wins. (It's wonderful when there are only two people singing knee to knee.)

To practice: Buy up all the musical albums and go to all the shows. Practice stopping at awkward moments.

To cheat: Introduce Adolph Green and Betty Comdon as Mr. and Mrs. Glutz.

Say Goodnight, Gracie

In this game, taught to me by Nancy Dunn, the object is to create a string of malapropisms.

Number of players: Two or more.

Tools: None.

To win: "Gracie" is a collective sport.

The play: In this game, you free-associate to the point of madness, guessing the words defined by your friends and adding new ones of your own.

For example: One person beings by saying, "Punk." Another player, it may be anyone, replies, "Isn't that the stuff they drink at weddings?"

"No, no," snaps a third, "That's punch."

"Isn't that a very masculine woman?" inquires a fourth.

"No," snarls a fifth, "That's a butch."

"Isn't that a place they keep rabbits?" chimes in another.

"No," says the first player, "That's a hutch."

The next person says, "Oh, isn't that like the little boy who put his finger in the dike?"

"No, no," another replies, "That's a klutz."

And so on. This can go on interminably until you get stuck. When you can't figure out what word your friend is defining, then you go to Phase 2 of the game, called

Oh, Goodnight, Gracie. In this phase, you introduce a totally off-the-wall word, having nothing whatsoever to do with the word that has gone before, but vaguely related to the definition preceding it. Since you might not get stuck in Phase 1 until late, say in a matter of days, you can also introduce Oh, Goodnight to avoid boredom.

Let us say that somebody, picking up from "klutz," says, "Isn't that a passionate sexual attraction?" Whereupon (being unable to think of "crush") you reply, "No, that's an affair." Stunned, the next player recovers, switches to Oh, Goodnight rules, and says, "Isn't that half man, half beast?" The next player responds: "No, that's a satyr." And you're off.

It is wise to play this game very fast or you might notice what you're doing.

To practice: Hang around with people who don't think in logical terms.

To cheat: If you can't win, you can't cheat.

Conversation

Conversation is a game based on drama and requiring an ability to play fast and loose with famous characters.

Number of players: The more the better.

Tools: None.

To win: Guess the secret identities.

The play: Two players leave the room. In the bathroom (or some other safe place), they choose two famous characters — from real life or literature, living or dead — to portray. The characters need not be people who knew each other — often it's better if they did not — but it's good if they had a common interest: Bob Dylan and Beethoven; Jackie Onassis and Cleopatra; Alfred Hitchcock and Edgar Allan Poe. The two players rejoin the group and proceed to have a conversation in character. The other players try to guess who they are. Anyone who guesses joins the conversation and says things to the two characters that are appropriate to their secret identities. Don't scream out their names, and join only if you know who both characters are. (Everyone, of course, cheats on this one.) If your guess is wrong, the two characters must somehow let you know, yet not divulge their secret identities. The game ends when everyone knows who everyone else is.

Get the Guest

Another of Jonathan Lipsky's inventions, guaranteed to liven up any party.

Number of players: Any number.

Tools: None.

To win: Bring in the most entertaining guest.

The play: Go out into the streets and literally "get a guest" to bring back to the party. Points are for the most interesting guest.

To cheat: Have Henry Kissinger waiting outside.

Impostor

A game that could as easily be called "job description" or "bureaucracy" because it takes its cue from our recently acquired ability to transform the more sublime aspects of language into the more ridiculous.

Number of players: Three or more.

Tools: None. A recent reading of the OSHA guidelines will get the brain into the proper state.

To win: The impostor wins by numbing his audience. The audience wins by guessing who he is.

The play: One person, IT, goes off by himself to decide what famous person, living or dead, fictional or real, he will pretend to be. Then he meditates awhile on how that person might describe himself or herself in the jargon of today's bureaucracy. (He recalls, for example, that the Nuclear Regulatory Commission, when referring to an explosion, calls it a "rapid disassembly.") Let us say he decides on Abraham Lincoln. He gets about ten minutes to rehearse his story, then he must return to the group. Once seated, he should begin:

> I was born in the Midwest to parents of the underclass. We lived in a single-unit dwelling made of inflammable material. I used self-facilitated transportation to get to the local educational center and, because I was highly motivated, received input in the evening hours using a lamp substitute. . . .

And so on. If someone in the audience should guess who the impostor is, he or she should ask a question. "Did you at any time discuss the relative merits of partition versus harmony before an assembly?" The impostor nods, letting the person know he has the right character.

The game continues with the impostor telling his story and the rest of the players asking questions until everyone in the group knows who it is. The first person to guess the truth becomes the next impostor.

To practice: Bone up on biography, then read any government publication. You won't be able to put a sentence together for weeks.

To cheat: As the impostor, you can cheat by having no person in mind whatsoever, talking nonsense, and merely agreeing with the first guess of the audience. This has the advantage of not wasting your gray cells on useless activity.

Bob and Carol, Ted and Alice

This one is a famous "icebreaker" from the 1930s which may break up more than your ice.

Number of players: An even number, four or more.

Tools: Sheets of paper, pins.

To win: Guess who you are and where your heart belongs.

The play: On arriving, guests are asked to turn their backs to the host and allow themselves to be pinned to a sheet of paper, on which is written the name of half of a famous couple. The othe half, presumably, is somewhere in the room. Once all the guests have arrived, they march about talking to everyone in the hope of finding their heart's desire. This chore is made doubly difficult by the fact that no one knows who they're looking for — a problem, I might add, that also exists outside the parlor. Players may ask each other any question at all except, "Who am I?"

Hosts should try to be a little imaginative in thinking up couples — how far they go depends on the limits of their friends. For example, you might invite Virginia Woolf and Vita Sackville West to your party in San Francisco, whereas in St. Louis you'd have to be content with Roy Rogers and Trigger. Do not let gender or reality stand in your way; the point is to get everyone talking, not to form more perfect unions.

To practice: Just do what you normally do at cocktail parties — wonder who you are and what you're doing there.

To cheat: Make a deal with that nice set of shoulders to your left such that if he (she) scratches your back, you'll scratch his (hers).

The Bucket of Water and the Shot Glass Tricks

I have no idea what these are doing in a book like this.

Number of players: Two or more.

Tools: A bucket of water, a broom, two shot glasses, a calling card, and a bottle of Jack Daniels.

To win: Figure out the bucket of water trick before you get too involved. Appreciate the shot glass trick.

The play: The bucket of water trick is as nasty as they come. My father, in his prime, used to play it on my brother and myself, and each of us found it entertaining as long as it was the other one who got fooled. You march into a room filled with people, bringing with you a bucket of water and a broom. You raise the bucket over your head and place in against the top of the door frame, then hold it there with the aid of the broom handle. People will stare at you. Let them. In about five minutes, say that you're getting a little tired and you'd like someone to hold the handle for a minute while you flex your arms. Some nice person will volunteer. Then he or she will be standing under a full bucket of water, holding it in place with a broom handle. You leave the person there. That is all there is.

The shot glass trick is not mean and, perhaps because of that, is more miraculous. Place a shot glass of whiskey on a table. The whiskey should fill the glass to the brim. Then fill an identical shot glass with water — to the brim — and place the calling card over the top. The card should cover the whole mouth of the glass. Then, very carefully, lift the glass of water and turn it upside down over the glass of whiskey, trying hard to hold the business card in place and not spill any water. Once the glasses are stable, pull the business card out a bit, so that a tiny hole is made through which the water can run into the whiskey glass. If all goes well — and do not be discouraged if it doesn't on the first try — something truly amazing will happen.

Buzz Numbers

A test of various mathematical powers and the ability to sustain silliness.

Number of players: Any number.

Tools: A working knowledge of arithmetic, a good memory, and the ability to ignore distraction while juggling numbers and nonsense words.

To win: Keep a clear head and a well-oiled tongue.

The play: Buzz Numbers can be played on various levels of complexity. Best to start with the simplest version. Players sit in a circle and a number — seven, let us say — is picked. They begin counting, clockwise, around the room. The first player says "one," the next says "two," and so on up to seven. But instead of "seven," the player whose turn it is must say "buzz." The players continue counting off in this manner, but whenever a multiple of seven — 14, 21, 28, and so on — is reached, the player whose turn has arrived must say "buzz." Players also must "buzz" at numbers that contain a seven — like 17. As players screw up they are eliminated, until one obsessively scrupulous player is left.

Variations: Increase the difficulty by playing several numbers at once, using different code words. If seven is "buzz," then five, for example, and all its multiples, can be "bang." And 35 — the product of five and seven — could be "bizz."

If you make it up to 57 and 75, the codes are "bang-buzz" and "buzz-bang," respectively.

Buzz Numbers can be played with as many numbers and code words as desired, depending on how long you can stand it.

stories

On the occasion of her eighty-second birthday, Mrs. Lucille Barret was kind enough to tell us a story. She had memorized this one and others forty years ago from "ladies' magazines" of the time in order to recite them to "ladies' club luncheons" at a dollar a recitation.

Briefly, it was the saga of a newly married women who is faced with the duty of meeting her husband's best friend's wife, a woman about whom the news is not good: she's beautiful, fashionable and from New York. It becomes clear to Dot, the bride, that her husband, Will, may be a honey but he doesn't understand the gravity of the situation. The crisis occurs when Will throws an impromptu party for Dot's birthday inviting, naturally, his friend and the by now famous wife. The house is a mess and Dot is wearing her worst "bungalow apron." After an awkward and inedible dinner cooked by the men and served on cracked china, the two women sit alone in the parlor trying desperately to make conversation. Finally they each confess their individual discomforts: "the wife" says she's embarrassed to drop in on Dot; Dot excuses her house. They both decry their husbands' ineptitude. All ends well: Dot has a new friend, Will surprises Dot with a brass electric teapot which he has bought with money saved for a fishing trip. As she leans tearfully against his "rough sleeve," she realizes marriage is a mixed bag.

The first story led to another — "The Night the Bikes Got Stolen," a nonfiction thriller by Dwayne Barret (Mrs. Barret's son), in which Mr. Barret, dressed in his shorts, chases two innocent paperboys down a surburban street at five a.m. Because of the stories, the day was especially blessed. "Like listening to radio," said one of us.

Therefore, my last offering is dedicated to Mrs. Barret and is called "stories," with a small "s" so you don't get threatened or highhanded. Just go out and memorize a story — James Thurber is a good place to begin — and the next time you get together with friends and family on a Sunday afternoon, tell it. Tell it to people on the bus during rush hour, tell it when the lights go out and the elevator breaks down and the plane won't leave on time. We'd all be grateful.

Answers

Answers to Whodunit? (p. 78)

A. Mary is a goldfish.

B. The man was a parachutist until his chute didn't open. The pack on his back contains the chute.

C. The man is a midget and can't reach the button for the 20th floor.

Long Division (p. 86)

Start with finding the answer. There are several things you know about the problem to begin with: First, you can see that it ends evenly, because of the zero remainder. Second, the second and fourth digits in the answer must be 0's because it was necessary to bring down two numbers from the dividend twice. Third, if you look at the first digit of the answer and notice how it multiplies by the divisor, you can see that it must be either an 8 or a 9 because its result is a high number. (How do you know the result is a high number? Because the result is three digits, and when it is subtracted from four digits, you get only two digits.) The same is true of the third digit in the answer. It, too, must be either an 8 or a 9 because of the high result. The last digit of the answer also must be an 8 or a 9 because it, too, is high, but in addition, its answer is also even and made up of four digits. So try it: Multiply 8×124 and then multiply 9×124 and see what you get. $9 \times 124 =$ a four-digit number. Now you know that the last digit is 9, and you also know that the first and third digits are 8's. Now you are on your own. It is also possible to do this problem without any division given.

Answer to Long Division (p. 86)

```
                    8 0 8 0 9
         124) 1 0 0 2 0 3 1 6
              9 9 2
              1 0 0 3
                9 9 2
                  1 1 1 6
                  1 1 1 6
                  0 0 0 0
```

About the Author and Illustrator

NORA GALLAGHER, a recognized Authority on parlor games, works as a West Coast correspondent for numerous publications, including Time, Life, and New West. In her brief, checkered career she has earned her living as an ad salesperson, a script supervisor on films, a stunt woman for the movie Billy Jack, and a teacher of schizophrenic children. Along the way, Ms. Gallagher has managed to acquire a reading knowledge of three dialects of ancient Greek — obviously good training for remembering the more arcane aspects of numerous parlor games. She was first introduced to these deceptively innocent amusements at a gathering of English majors, where she quickly became intimidated by a discussion of George Eliot that lofted toward the esoteric. "Then all of a sudden," she remembers, "they turned out the lights and started crawling around in the dark, grappling with each other." Later on, she discovered, this group grope was actually a parlor game, Murder #3. "I immediately understood the real appeal of this game and others," she said. "It is a good opportunity for everyone to pounce on people they've always dreamed of grabbing. Once the game got going, who cared about the murderer?"

ANNIE GUSMAN, a native of New York City, works as a free-lance illustrator of books and other publications. A graduate of the Rhode Island School of Design, Ms. Gusman now lives in Boston. Recently she has illustrated children's books, including Up the Down Elevator, by Norma Farber.

Although Ms. Gusman claims that she was too busy drawing to enjoy parlor games when she was young, she now thinks that a game like Mental Strip Poker might be amusing.